THE SOLDIER THROUGH THE AGES
THE WORLD WAR 1
TOMMY
MARTIN WINDROW

Martin Windrow

Illustrated by
Richard Hook

Franklin Watts
London   New York   Toronto   Sydney

First published in Great Britain in 1986 by
Franklin Watts Limited
12a Golden Square
London W1

First published in the USA by
Franklin Watts Inc.
387 Park Avenue South
New York
N.Y. 10016

First published in Australia by
Franklin Watts Australia
14 Mars Road
Lane Cove
NSW 2066

UK edition ISBN: 0 86313 299 5
US edition ISBN: 0-531-10083-9
Library of Congress Catalog Card
No: 85-50764

Designed by James Marks

Printed in Belgium ℳ

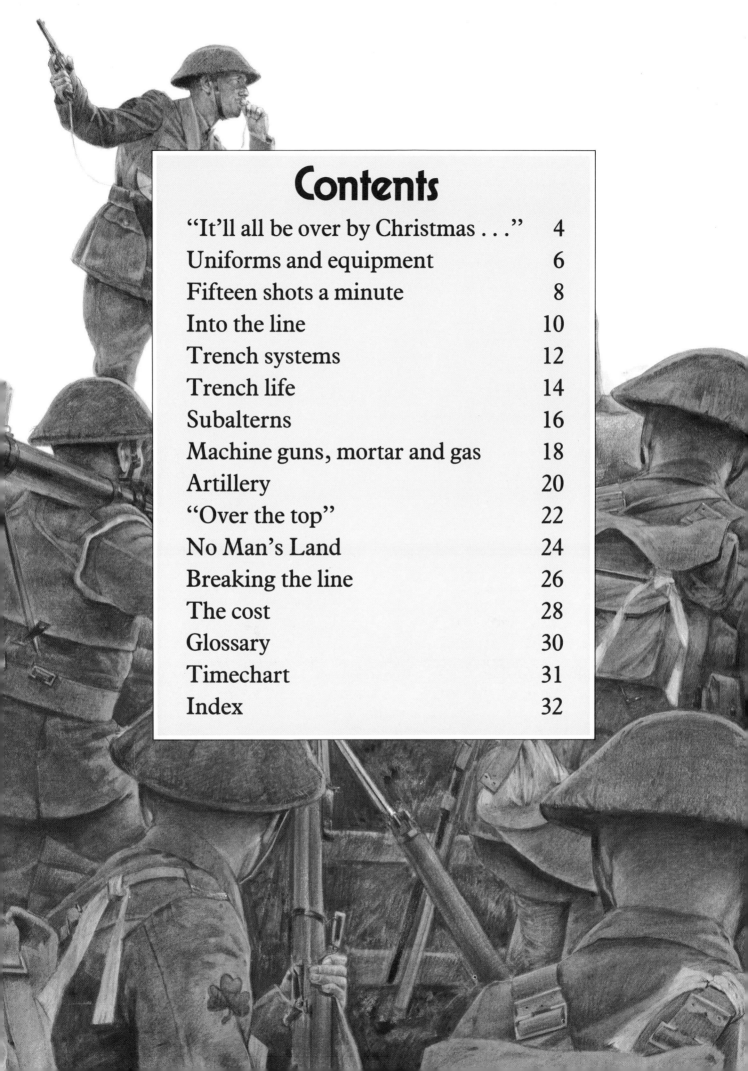

Contents

"It'll all be over by Christmas..."

In the summer of 1914 an assassination in faraway Bosnia and a complicated tangle of European political alliances plunged the great powers into World War I. Without any clear idea why, and completely unaware of the horrors that were to follow, the peoples of Britain, France, Russia, Belgium and later Italy found themselves at war with Germany, Austria and Turkey.

The armies of 1914 were led by generals who mostly had learned their trade in colonial campaigns. Some still believed in the saber-charge by horse cavalry as a battle-winning weapon. They had no idea that they were about to fight a stalemated war with static front lines, dominated by massed machine guns, heavy artillery that could fire huge shells from far beyond the horizon, poison gas, flamethrowers and tanks.

At the outset all was confidence. Britain's first battles in France and Belgium were fought by her pre-war Regular Army. Although magnificently trained, it soon proved too small in numbers for its task. In September 1914 Britain's war minister, Lord Kitchener, called for 100,000 civilian volunteers; in three weeks he got half a million. Everyone believed that the war would be "over by Christmas," and was anxious to "do his bit," out of patriotism or the hope of excitement.

Some had more practical reasons. Laborers and clerks struggling to provide for families on wages of a few shillings a week were attracted by Army pay of at least a shilling a day. (Army Service Corps drivers could earn six times this amount.) Some men enlisted with large groups of friends and workmates, on condition they could serve together. When one of these "Pals' Battalions" was wiped out, a whole village might be widowed and orphaned in a single day.

By January 1916 a draft law had to be passed in order to fill up the ranks. For the first time British men could be made to serve in the army whether they wanted to or not. Some 2,466,350 volunteers had enlisted by then; a further 2,504,200 draftees were called up between 1916 and 1918.

Soldiers were nicknamed "Tommies" after Thomas Atkins, a made-up name for a soldier in a sample Army account book of 1829. After a few months of rather unrealistic training, by men who usually knew little more of modern war than the recruits, the Tommies were shipped across the Channel to France.

Uniforms and equipment

Since 1902 the British soldier had worn a uniform of drab khaki to blend in with his surroundings. Badges worn on his uniform were at first limited to the cap and shoulder insignia of his regiment, and to rank and length-of-service stripes.

As the war drew on, however, it was found to be useful to add new kinds of badges. By 1918 his uniform was the background for a vivid and complicated display of badges, stripes and insignia, from which his exact unit, rank, experience and special skills could all be told at a glance. The years 1916–18 saw the birth of many kinds of badges which are still worn by the world's armies today.

The *division* of about 18,700 men was the largest unit to wear its own distinguishing badge. The infantry was divided into three *brigades* of about 4,000 men; and each brigade had four *battalions* of 800 to 1,000 men. (Battalions of several regiments were assembled into a brigade – the regiment did not serve together as a single unit in battle.) The battalion had four *companies* of about 250 men; and the company was the smallest unit ever to wear its own distinguishing insignia (though not all of them did). A company had four *platoons* of about 60 men, each led by a junior officer; and NCOs led *sections* of about 15 men.

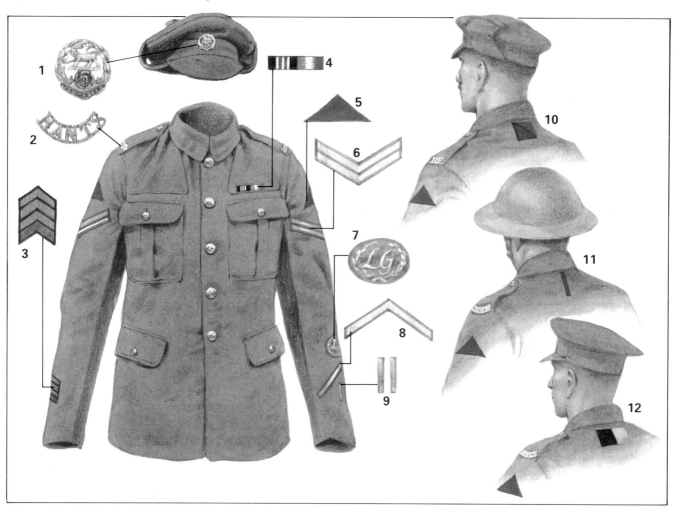

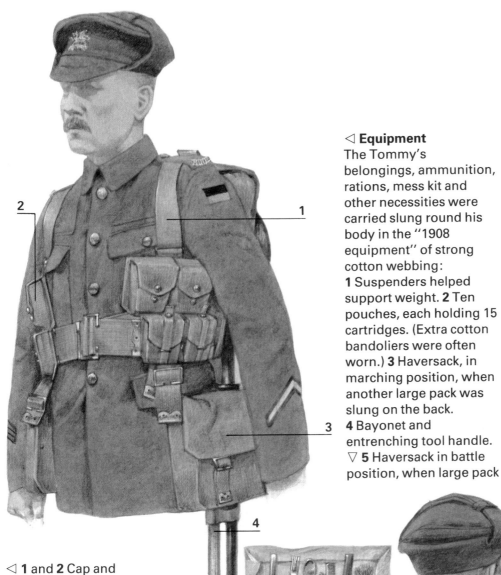

Equipment

The Tommy's belongings, ammunition, rations, mess kit and other necessities were carried slung round his body in the "1908 equipment" of strong cotton webbing:
1 Suspenders helped support weight. **2** Ten pouches, each holding 15 cartridges. (Extra cotton bandoliers were often worn.) **3** Haversack, in marching position, when another large pack was slung on the back.
4 Bayonet and entrenching tool handle.
▽ **5** Haversack in battle position, when large pack was laid aside. Contents included towel, washing and shaving kit, bully beef, crackers; under the flap a waterproof groundsheet, and, attached to the straps, mess tins in a cover.
6 Bag for early type of "PH" gas masks.
7 Canteen.
8 Entrenching tool head and its case.
9 Pouch detail.
10 Mills hand grenade, often carried in pockets.

Full pack with spare clothes weighed about 77 lb (35 kg) in winter; a greatcoat soaked in rain and mud could weigh an additional 40 lb (18 kg).

◁ **1** and **2** Cap and shoulder badges, Royal Hampshire Regiment.
3 One service chevron for each year overseas – red for 1914 service.
4 Ribbons for Military Medal (gallantry) and 1914 Star (campaign medal). **5** 29th Division.
6 Corporal's chevrons.
7 Lewis gunner's "skill at arms" badge.
8 Good conduct stripe.
9 Two wound stripes.

"Battle badges" were often worn on the back. Shape sometimes indicated the brigade, and color the battalion.
10 2nd Royal Fusiliers, 86th Bde., 29th Div.
11 1st Border Regt., 87th Bde., 29th Div.
12 2nd Royal Hampshire Regt., 88th Bde., 29th Div.

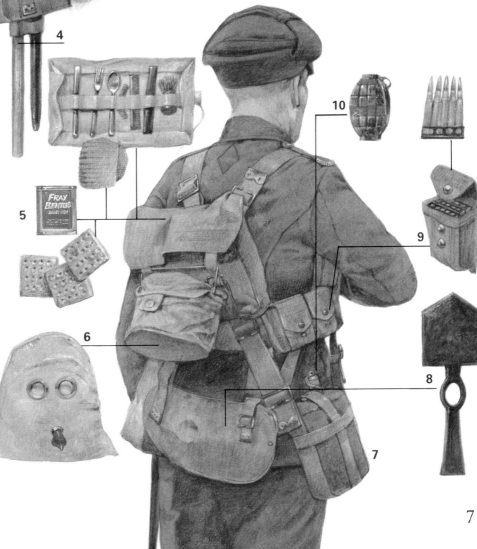

Fifteen shots a minute

At the battle of Mons in August 1914 a crack German unit was driven off by a British unit with such heavy losses that the Germans believed that they had come up against a machine-gun battalion. In fact, they had attacked a British infantry battalion of pre-war professional soldiers armed only with rifles. But the "old sweats" of the Regular Army who went to France in 1914 were trained to use their rifles with such skill that the effect was not unlike machine-gun fire. Each man was trained to fire fifteen aimed shots in a minute – and that included time to reload.

Their weapon was the .303-inch (7.92-mm) caliber Lee-Enfield bolt-action magazine rifle. All World War I armies used bolt-action rifles. They were well designed, very strongly made, and so accurate that a marksman could, in theory, hit a man-sized target a mile away. At the usual battle ranges of a few hundred yards they shot straight and fast.

The Lee-Enfield was loaded with ten brass cartridges at a time. These were kept in spring clips of five rounds together. The Tommy opened the rifle by turning and pulling back a "bolt," so called from its

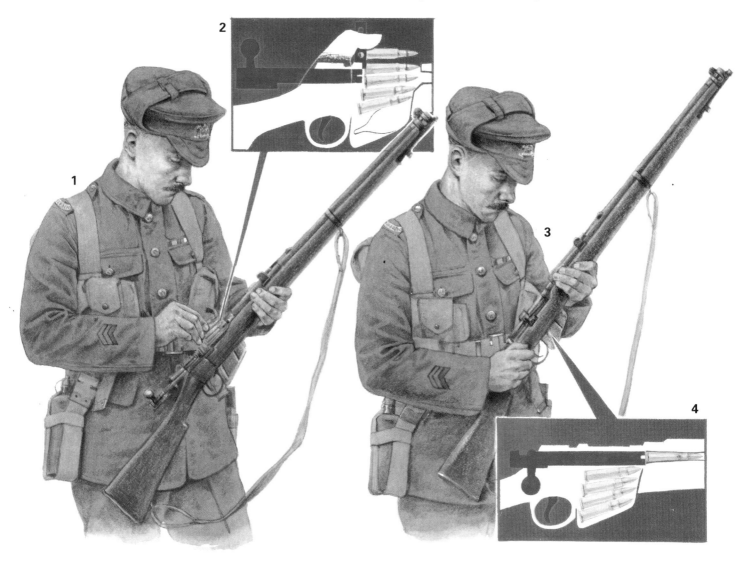

8

resemblance to an ordinary door bolt. He pressed the cartridges down from their clips into a spring-loaded compartment – the magazine – fitted below the breech of the rifle. This closing of the bolt automatically stripped the top cartridge out of the magazine and pushed it into the barrel; it also cocked the spring-loaded firing pin inside the bolt. After firing, the soldier opened and closed the bolt again; this flipped out the empty cartridge and pushed the next one into place. He could keep firing as fast as he could aim, pull the trigger and work the bolt.

▽ **Loading and firing**
1 The bolt is open and the clip of cartridges held ready. Two clips were loaded one after another.
2 The clip is fitted into a slot above the breech. The Tommy pushes the rounds down out of the clip, against the spring inside the magazine.
3 He pushes the bolt forward, turning the handle down to lock it.
4 This pushes the top cartridge into the barrel, ready to fire.

5 He fires. Veterans often used their second finger on the trigger, keeping the index finger hooked round the bolt handle for speed of recocking.
6 and **7** He recocks the rifle by pushing the bolt handle up, pulling it back, then pushing it forward and down again. The empty cartridge flies out, and the magazine spring pushes the next up into place.

5

7

6

9

Into the line

The first weeks of fighting saw sweeping movements by great armies. The Germans advanced deep into France and Belgium. But by October 1914 a new pattern was emerging. The armies slowed down and finally came to a halt, facing one another. The new weapons which they were meeting for the first time – massed machine guns and long-range heavy artillery – made movement so incredibly costly in lives that they were forced to dig trenches for shelter. The trenches were extended until they joined up in a single belt, running 475 miles (765 km) from the North Sea to the Swiss borders.

In this long strip of countryside, only about 30 miles (50 km) wide, the Tommy was to fight his most terrible war. More and more men and guns were brought into this Western Front war zone. The defenders enjoyed all the advantages, and attacks against enemy trench lines became almost suicidal. The generals, frustrated by this stalemate and by demands for "action" from politicians, newspapers and civilians at home, kept repeating their failed attacks, at hideous cost. Moreover, since the Germans had advanced into their enemies' territory, they could afford to sit tight for long periods and let the Allies take the risks of attacking.

One offensive after another was launched across this narrow strip of land, but there was scarcely any change in the opposing front lines until the summer of 1918. Shellfire pounded the earth to dust, and rain turned it into mud. Forests were reduced to ashes and villages to rubble.

The Tommies struggled and endured in a nightmare landscape.

British units usually spent about a week at a time in the trenches, though it could be a month or even longer in times of emergency. A "tour" in the front line was usually followed by a week or so in support, close to the front, and a week or two "resting" (actually, doing hard physical labor) in the rear. The Tommy might get a week's home leave once a year. A Royal Warwickshires officer reckoned that in 1916 he spent 101 days in the line, 120 days in support within a day's march of the Front, 73 days "resting" and the remaining 71 days on training courses, in hospital, on leave or traveling. Units were moved from sector to sector at frequent intervals.

▽ Fresh from England, Tommies march up to the front line. (Trucks and horse-drawn wagons were mostly kept for moving supplies.) This company is passing a 9.2-in (23-cm) howitzer in the heavy artillery lines a few miles back from the trenches. From here the artillery shelled the enemy trenches – and enemy guns, when they could be pin-pointed by observers in aircraft. Such guns had ranges of nearly 10 miles (16 km), and could strike deep into the enemy's rear areas.

Trench systems

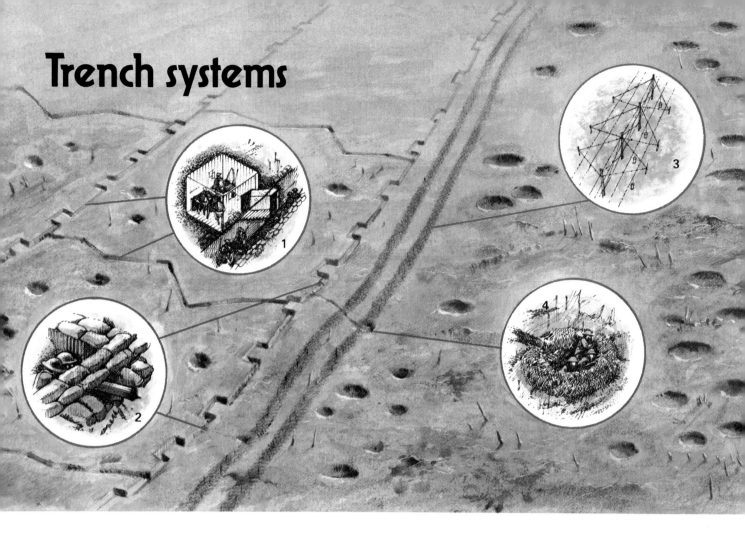

Trenches were not simply ditches dug at random, but carefully planned systems. On each side of "No Man's Land" – which might by anything from 50 to 500 paces wide – there were usually three lines of trenches. (The Germans, who prepared more for static defense than attack, had up to ten lines in some sectors.)

The front line was the fire trench. As the first line of defense and the jumping-off point for attackers, it was the best fortified and most alertly guarded. Some way behind was the second or support trench, with most of the dugouts for command posts, medical aid posts and trench supplies. Here men waited in case they were needed to support the front-line trench. Some way behind this was the third reserve trench. An infantry battalion "in the line" held a section of all three lines, one behind the other.

The trenches were about 6½ ft (2 m) deep, including the thick parapet of sandbags laid on the surface of the ground at the front. A shelf of earth and sandbags, the fire step, ran along the front wall, so men could climb up to shoot over the parapet when necessary. Wooden duckboards were laid on the bottom of the trench, in the vain hope of keeping the feet out of the worst of the mud. Shallow "funk holes" were scraped in the walls, where men sheltered from the weather and tried to keep out of the way of the constant traffic up and down the trench. The walls were lined with timber, wire netting and sandbags to keep them from crumbling in the rain and shellfire, but the Tommies had to work constantly to repair them. (A wartime song included the line: "*Most of France's in a sandbag, and the rest of it's all over me . . .*")

The trenches were dug in "dog-tooth" shape, with sections about ten paces long divided up by buttresses of earth and sandbags. This prevented shell blast, or the fire of attackers, from sweeping along whole lines of trench with murderous results. There were also communication trenches to enable men to get back and forth between the three lines of trenches under cover.

Barbed wire was laid in several belts in front of the trenches, at least 20 paces wide, so attackers could not throw grenades from its forward edge over into the trenches. It was laid in horizontal "fences" at several heights, then thickened up with diagonal lines until – with constant improvement and repair – it formed a chaotic entanglement. Pebble-and-tin-can rattles were hung in it to warn of the approach of enemy patrols at night.

△ **1** British dugouts were anything from 6–15 ft (2–4.5 m) square, up to 15 ft (4.5 m) below trench level.
2 Machine guns were sited so that lines of fire met in a crossfire at the front edge of the wire.
3 Wire was strung on iron or wooden stakes. Going out at night to repair it was a dangerous, hated and frequent duty for the Tommy in the front line.
4 Another nerve-racking job was lying out ahead of the trenches in wired-over listening posts, guarding against stealthy enemy attacks.
5 German dugouts were sometimes as much as 40 ft (12 m) deep, dug down into solid chalk, their several floors accommodating whole platoons of men, with

bunks, electric light and other comforts. In 1916–18 the German front-line trenches were often only thinly held, with most men waiting in safety further back and far underground.
6 Concrete "pill boxes" for machine-gun crews strengthened the front line.
7 German mortar pit, its E-shape dividing the mortar crew from the stock of bombs to limit damage if hit by an enemy shell.
8 Tunnel under No Man's Land. Both sides dug these; when the tunnel reached the enemy line it was filled with explosive and set off, blowing a vast crater to coincide with an infantry attack.
9 Sniper lying hidden in No Man's Land.

Trench life

Trench conditions varied from place to place, but were never comfortable and almost always unspeakably wretched. With no chance to bathe or change for days or weeks at a time, the Tommies crawled with lice. Sniper fire made movement above ground suicidal, so human waste and unburied corpses covered the war zone, attracting millions of rats and flies. The smell of death never dispersed. Sickness was rife. In the rainy British sector in Flanders 12 in (30 cm) of mud in the trenches was normal, and thigh-deep mud not uncommon. Men who slipped into shellholes drowned horribly in sucking, soupy mud. Perpetually wet boots caused trench foot, a condition which often meant that toes had to be amputated.

Living crouched in a stinking ditch, the wet, cold, tired, tensed-up soldiers had few comforts. Mail from home was regular and welcome, and so was the small rum ration. In those days most men smoked, and the Army issued 30 cigarettes a week free. Food was cold and unappetizing: hard crackers, stale bread, jam, and canned "Maconochie's" stew (mostly turnips). Tea made with chlorinated water was carried up in gasoline cans, which hardly improved the flavor!

▷ In the trenches men were awake and working most of the time. Each dawn and dusk they "stood to" – manning the parapet for an hour, as most attacks came at those times. Inspections and snatched meals were the only breaks from hours of hard work. Trenches needed constant repair, and stores had to be carried forward each night. After dark some men stood sentry duty; others worked on; and about one man in three got a chance to try to sleep – despite cold, noise and constant traffic – in cramped funk holes scraped in the trench walls.

Subalterns

The young platoon and company commanders – subalterns – who led the Tommies shared most of the squalor and all of the danger. (Staff officers were seldom seen in the front line, however.) One privilege for officers was sleeping and doing their paperwork in dugouts, tiny caves dug below the trench walls. Dank, filthy, smoke-filled, and giving no great protection from shells, they at least kept out the rain. Officers tried to make them homely with small comforts like record players and pin-ups.

Officers usually came from a private school or university background, followed by brief training. Aged from 18 to 25, they were mostly cheerful, kind and anxious to do their duty both to their country and their men. They were taught to "lead from the front" and they died in huge numbers. A lieutenant's life at the Front was often measured in only weeks. In one battalion it was found that officers were killed five times as fast as privates.

War brought men of very different social classes closer together than ever before. The shared danger bred respect, even affection.

▷ Officers question an enemy prisoner after a trench raid and check regimental shoulder straps cut from enemy casualties. Raids by small parties were common. The generals wanted information about enemy units facing them. They also thought it important not to let the enemy, or their own men, get used to a "quiet life." Raids meant perhaps hours of silent stalking, followed by a short, savage hand-to-hand fight with pistols, knives, grenades and handmade clubs. Faces were blackened, helmets replaced by knitted caps, and all noisy or awkward equipment left behind. The NCO (right) wears padded cloth armor with grenade pockets: it might stop bomb splinters, but not bullets.

Machine guns, mortar and gas

The most important new weapon of the war, and the one which forced the armies to stop where they were and dig themselves underground, was the machine gun. The Allied generals made their greatest mistake in not taking it seriously enough from the first weeks of fighting. For infantry to attack across open ground against trenches defended by plentiful machine guns was simply mass suicide. The Tommies advanced into a sort of invisible "meat grinder," each rank falling as they reached the machine guns' line of fire. Firing hundreds of times each minute, and set up in advance aimed at the enemy's parapet, two machine guns could halt a thousand men. Six could destroy a brigade. At Loos, in September 1915, twelve attacking British battalions – about 10,000 men – lost 8,246 in just three and a half hours, mainly to machine-gun fire. Both sides used them of course. But since it was usually the Tommies and the French soldiers, or *poilus*, who were doing the attacking, they suffered worst.

Both sides also devised weapons to kill the enemy even when he was below ground. Trench mortars were simple weapons which fired heavy bombs at a high angle, lobbing them down into the enemy trenches. They were so slow they could be seen in the air.

◁ A British gas sentry sounds the alarm on a shellcase gong as gas seeps heavily into his trench. It formed pools, lying in wait for careless soldiers for some days. Early gas masks, soaked in chemicals, were cumbersome and not very efficient; they did not protect the body from skin burns.

△ German Maxim machine gun. Linked, 200-round belts allowed almost continuous firing at 600 rounds per minute.

▷ A German crew loads a yellow cross gas bomb into a trench mortar. Alternative 200-lb (90-kg) explosive bombs sent shockwaves through the ground for nearly a mile.

One hideous new weapon was poison gas. First used by Germany in 1915, it was either released from canisters on to a favorable wind, or fired into enemy lines in shells. A badly gassed man took days or even weeks to die in pitiful agony. His skin burned away in huge blisters, while his throat and lungs rotted from the inside. The burned, blinded sufferer died at last from suffocation, or from drowning as his dissolving lungs filled with fluid.

Artillery

Artillery was the most practical weapon to use against trenches and the most dangerous and terrifying scourge of the infantry. To prepare for an infantry attack, huge numbers of guns pounded the trenches to cut the barbed wire and smash machine-gun posts. The weight of fire was the greatest ever known. By mid-1917 barrages lasted for days at a time. Several thousand guns, lined up one every six paces, fired nearly 5 tons (5,000 kg) of shells for every yard of front line. On a single day in September 1917 British guns fired one million rounds. Even in "quiet" periods a constant harassing fire of a few shells an hour kept the infantry on edge and caused a steady drain of casualties. Any sign of unusual activity spotted by observers in balloons and aircraft would bring down a rain of accurate shellfire. Even "friendly" artillery was dangerous: shells often dropped short among their own infantry during an advance.

◁ Tommies frantically dig out a comrade buried by a shellburst. Heavy guns, like the German 16.5-in (42-cm) howitzer, sent 1-ton (1,000-kg) shells 6 miles (9.5 km) and made craters the size of a house. Whole platoons were buried alive, apart from the men torn to shreds by huge, red-hot steel shards or turned inside out by the blast. Air-bursts rained steel shrapnel from above the trenches. In long bombardments men often went mad with fear, noise and blast.

"Over the top"

Before Tommies were sent "over the top" in a major attack, great movements of men and supplies were needed. Enemy observers often spotted these, so the Germans were warned in advance. If the artillery barrage failed to cut the enemy's wire or smash his defenses, the attackers would face a hail of bullets and impossible obstacles. Sometimes they found that guns were trained in advance on the gaps they had to cut in their own wire.

Commanders quickly lost touch with attacking troops: telephone wires were cut by gunfire, and runners got lost or killed. More men were sent forward to certain death through simple ignorance of what was happening. On July 1, 1916, the first day of the Somme offensive, 57,470 Tommies fell.

▽ To the shrilling of their officer's whistle, Tommies clamber up ladders to the parapet. They carry not only their own gear, but extra ammunition, tools, wire, empty sandbags and other supplies: after capturing the shell-torn enemy line, they must fortify and hold it against inevitable counterattacks. Most carry some 75 lb (34 kg) – half their own weight, and far too much for speed and agility in combat. One has a Lewis light machine gun, one of four in his company. Steel helmets were usually covered with sacking to prevent tell-tale reflections. Rags tied to webbing remind men which group they are meant to follow in the confusion.

No Man's Land

Some of the wounded, left lying helpless in shellholes or hanging on barbed wire, were rescued at night by heroic stretcher-bearers; but many died lonely, wretched deaths. Searches or patrols by night amid the filth and corpses of No Man's Land were always nerve-racking. It was easy to get lost; any noise brought down enemy flares and probing machine-gun fire; and returning patrols might be fired on by their own jumpy sentries.

Breaking the line

Very heavy fighting in 1918 saw the Germans at first pushing the Allies back many miles; then they were brought to a halt and finally pushed back by the British and French armies now reinforced by newly arrived American troops. On November 11, 1918 the Germans were forced to agree to an armistice or cease-fire.

In 1918 both sides used new tactics. Instead of trying to take whole lines of Allied trenches, the Germans sent specially trained and heavily armed "storm" units against weak points. Punching through, they advanced into the rear areas to knock out the artillery. Allied strongpoints, cut off and without artillery support, were "mopped up" later by other troops.

The Allies, supported by aircraft, spearheaded attacks with tanks. These armorplated tracked vehicles could burst through barbed wire and climb over trenches; their guns could knock out machine-gun posts. The Tommies followed them, fanning out through the gaps they made to "roll up" German trenches from end to end.

▷ A Sopwith Camel fighter flies low over advancing Allied tanks and infantry, ready to support them with machine guns and small bombs. In 1914–15 planes were used only for scouting; in 1916–17 new types and new tactics led to great air battles; and in 1917–18 there was increasing use of planes to "strafe" the enemy on the ground. This was particularly true during the German advance of spring 1918 and the Allied push which followed that summer.

Tanks proved their worth at Cambrai in November 1917: 450 tanks broke through enemy defenses – but the high command had doubted their capabilities and had not supported them with sufficient infantry to move forward through the gap. By late 1918 the lesson had been learned, and tanks led the final Allied advance with plenty of infantry following close behind.

The cost

World War I cost the lives of about eight and a half million servicemen of all nations. Of these, *more than one million* were British. Of every hundred British males under the age of 45, about nine were killed in the war. On the main Western Front, in France and Belgium, 677,515 British soldiers were killed in action or died from wounds, and a further 1,837,613 were wounded.

These appalling figures mean that of all the British soldiers sent to France and Belgium – *including* tens of thousands of combat troops who never got into battle and tens of thousands of men in non-combatant units far from the Front – 13.4 per cent were killed, and 36.4 per cent were wounded. When a Tommy got off the boat in France, he had a fifty-fifty chance of being killed or wounded.

The men who survived and rose to senior rank before the next world war swore that never again would a British army be sent into such hopeless slaughter. One trench war was enough; in the future the key would be movement. In World War II, for all its horror, the number of British soldiers killed was less than a quarter of the number killed on the Western Front alone in 1914–18.

Glossary

Balloon Hydrogen-filled balloons were used to carry artillery observers aloft.

Bandolier Simple cloth shoulder belt for ammunition.

Barrage Period of concentrated artillery fire; always used to prepare target for planned infantry attack.

Battalion Unit of about 1,000 men, led by a lieutenant-colonel.

Bayonet Knife-like weapon which could be clipped to muzzle of rifle for close combat.

Brigade Formation of four battalions; total strength about 4,100 men commanded by a brigadier-general.

Cartridge Rifle ammunition: a brass tube holding the bullet, explosive, and a percussion cap which set it off when struck by the spring-loaded firing pin released by the trigger.

Chevron V-shaped embroidered cloth rank stripe worn on sleeves by NCOs.

Chlorine Chemical used both to purify dirty water and, in 1914–18, to make poison gas.

Company Unit about 250 strong, led by a captain. Four made up a battalion.

Division Military formation of three infantry brigades plus supporting units commanded by a major-general and totaling 18,700 men.

Duckboards Wooden planking, like flat ladders, laid on trench floor to give a dry footing.

Dugout Artificial cave or underground room, dug below trench walls.

Entrenching tool Small combination pick-and-shovel tool carried by soldiers.

Flamethrower Weapon invented in 1914–18 for clearing trenches and pill boxes: a portable tank of oil with a hose that squirted a fine spray of blazing drops in a tongue of flame many yards long.

Hand grenade Small hand-thrown bomb, powerful enough to kill a group of men.

Haversack Small canvas pack for personal gear, usually carried slung on the hip.

Howitzer Heavy artillery gun of large caliber which fired at a high angle to lob shells on to the target.

Lewis gun Light machine-gun fed from round pans of cartridges.

Lieutenant Junior officer, usually in command of a platoon.

Machine gun Mechanical, tripod-mounted weapon fed by canvas ammunition belts or spring-loaded metal magazines, and capable of firing continuously at a rate of hundreds of shots a minute.

Mills bomb Type of British grenade.

NCO Non-commissioned officer – senior soldier holding rank of lance-corporal, corporal or sergeant.

No Man's Land The contested ground between two facing lines of trenches.

Parapet The built-up wall of sandbags in front of a trench.

PH helmet Gas mask issued in 1915-16, made of cloth impregnated with a chemical which neutralized poison gas. PH stands for Phenate Hexane.

Pill box Small concrete bunker above ground which sheltered machine-gun crews from enemy fire.

Platoon Unit of about 60 men, led by a junior officer; four made up a company.

Poilu Literally, "hairy one" – the French slang for a soldier, the equivalent of the British Tommy.

Regiment Historic unit of British Army, usually named after the county where it recruited its battalions. Only individual battalions went to war, assembled into brigades. The whole parent regiment never took the field as a fighting unit.

Sandbag Small sack, actually filled with earth rather than sand, used to build field fortifications.

Shoulder straps German tunic shoulder straps bore colored emblems and numbers which identified their unit.

Sniper Expert marksman who picked off unwary soldiers who poked their heads above the parapet.

Storm battalion German unit, specially trained to fight across enemy trenches.

Strafe Attack, particularly from the air: slang, from the German word for punishment.

Tank Heavy armored track-laying vehicle fitted with guns; developed by the British in World War I as a means of crossing wire entanglements and trenches under fire. "Tank" was its code-name during secret trials: the Army pretended these large steel boxes were a new type of water tank.

Trench mortar Simple, wide-barreled, short-range gun used for lobbing very large shells short distances.

Webbing Cotton canvas belting used to make soldiers' belts and pouches.

Western Front The main war zone in northern France and Belgium, 1914–18.

1914 *June* Austrian Archduke assassinated at Sarajevo. *August* General outbreak of war; Germans invade Belgium and France through northern France; checked at Mons. *September* French counter-attack on the Marne. Germans defeat Russians at Tannenberg. *October* 1st Battle of Ypres. *December* Western Front stabilized.

1915 *January* French offensive fails. *March* British attack fails at Neuve Chapelle. *April* German attack fails at 2nd Battle of Ypres; Allies land at Gallipoli. *May* Second French offensive. *September* British attack fails at Loos. *December* Allies forced to withdraw from Gallipoli.

1916 *January* Britain introduces conscription. *February–July* German offensive at Verdun held off by French. *July–November* British-French offensive on Somme repulsed by Germans.

1917 *March* Germans shorten their line by voluntarily retreating to strong Hindenberg Line defenses. Russian Revolution; Tsar abdicates. *April* USA joins Allies. Allied offensive opens: French repulsed on Aisne and in Champagne with heavy loss; mutinies follow. Limited British success at Arras, Vimy Ridge. *August–November* 3rd Battle of Ypres; Passchendaele. 300,000 British casualties. Tanks used at Cambrai. *December* Russia makes peace.

1918 *March* Successful German offensive. Allies forced to retreat. *April* Germans halted. *July* Supreme Allied C-in-C, Marshal Foch, halts German advance on Marne. American troops go into battle. *August–November* Successful Allied counter-offensive. *October* Turkey makes peace. *November* Germany and Austria accept armistice conditions.

Index